THANKFULNESS

by Cynthia Roberts

Published in the United States of America by The Child's World®
1980 Lookout Drive • Mankato, MN 56003-1705 • 800-599-READ • www.childsworld.com

The Child's World®: Mary Berendes, Publishing Director; Katherine Stevenson, Editor
The Design Lab: Kathy Petelinsek, Art Director; Julia Goozen, Design and Page Production

Photo Credits: © Brand X Pictures: 5. 21; © Corbis: cover; © David M. Budd Photography: 9, 11, 13; © iStockphoto.com/
Ana Abejon: 15; © pixland/Corbis: 7; © Sean Justice/Corbis: 17; © Steve Chenn/Corbis: 19

Library of Congress Cataloging-in-Publication Data
Roberts, Cynthia, 1960–
  Thankfulness / by Cynthia Roberts.
    p. cm. — (Learn about values)
  ISBN 978-1-59296-677-6 ISBN 1-59296-677-2 (library bound : alk. paper)
  1. Gratitude—Juvenile literature. 2. Values—Juvenile literature. I. Title. II. Series.
  BJ1533.G8R63 2006
  179'.9—dc22   2006000967

CONTENTS

What Is Thankfulness?

There are many things to be happy about! Maybe you have a cute new baby sister. Maybe your grandma has moved closer to you. Maybe someone has baked your **favorite** cookies. Thankfulness means having good "thank-you" feelings about something. When you are thankful, you feel **grateful** for what you have.

Thankfulness means feeling lucky to have certain things in your life.

5

Thankfulness at School

It is lunchtime at school. You cannot wait to eat your sandwich. It is your favorite kind. You sit down and open your lunch. Your sandwich is not there! You forgot to put it in your lunch bag. Your friend sees what happened. She gives you half of her sandwich. You are thankful for your friend's kindness.

A friend's help can make you feel thankful.

Thankfulness for Someone's Kindness

You and your friends are racing on the playground. You fall and hurt your arm. The school nurse cleans your arm. She puts on a bandage. She talks to you about how you are feeling. She makes you feel better. You are thankful she is there!

We feel thankful when someone takes good care of us.

9

Thankfulness for Your Friends

Your best friend is great. You do everything together. She likes to do the same things you do. She laughs at your jokes. When something is bothering you, she listens while you talk. She cheers you up when you are sad. You are thankful to have a friend like her!

Thank you for being such a good friend!

Thankfulness for Your Parents

Your mom and dad work hard at their jobs. They keep your house clean. They make sure you have good food to eat. They help you stay safe. They do things to make you happy. You are thankful that your parents take care of you. You are thankful that they love you.

You can be thankful for people who love you.

Thankfulness for Your Family

Sometimes you fight with your sister. Sometimes you get mad at your mom and dad. Even so, you love your family. They cheer you up when you are sad. They help you when you are scared. They teach you new things. You are thankful that they are your family!

We feel thankful that our families are there for us.

Thankfulness and Your Neighborhood

In the summer, you go swimming at the pool. You check out books from the library. You and your friends play in the park. These are great places to go! You know that some kids are not so lucky. Their neighborhoods do not have such nice places. You are thankful to live in a neighborhood that does.

Thankfulness means noticing the nice things around us.

Thankfulness for Someone's Help

Sometimes people go out of their way to help others. Maybe someone has helped you with your reading. Perhaps somebody helped you learn something new. Maybe a neighbor helped you fix your bike. Maybe a friend cheered you up when you were sad. You feel thankful when someone does something nice for you!

Sometimes people's help can really mean a lot!

Thankfulness for Everything

Take a look at the people, places, and things around you. What do you have to be thankful for? You can show thankfulness by saying "thank you." You can give someone a thank-you hug. Or you can do something nice for someone else! Thankfulness makes the world a brighter place.

There are lots of things to be thankful for!

glossary

favorite
When you like something best, it is your favorite.

grateful
Feeling grateful is feeling glad that something good has happened.

books

Chessen, Betsey, and Pamela Chanko. *Thank You!* New York: Scholastic, 1998.

Chorao, Kay. *The Book of Giving: Poems of Thanks, Praise and Celebration*. New York: Dutton, 1995.

Milgrim, David. *Thank You, Thanksgiving*. New York: Clarion, 2003.

Stuart, Carole, and Arthur Robins. *The Thank You Book*. New York: Four Walls Eight Windows, 2003.

web sites

Visit our Web page for links about character education and values:
http://www.childsworld.com/links

Note to parents, teachers, and librarians:
We routinely check our Web links to make sure they're safe,
active sites—so encourage your readers to check them out!

index

about the author

Even as a child, Cynthia Roberts knew she wanted to be a writer. She is always working to involve kids in reading and writing, and she loves spending time in the children's section of the library or bookstore. Cynthia enjoys gardening, traveling, and having fun with friends and family.

24